# Clean-Up

Catherine James
Illustrated by Abby Carter

RIGBY

Today we cleaned up our house.

Dad cleaned up.

Mum cleaned up.

Gran cleaned up.

Grandad cleaned up.

I cleaned up my room.
I put my old clothes in boxes.

I cleaned up the playroom.
I put my old toys in boxes.

TOYS

TOYS

Then we had a sale.

We sold all our old things.

We made our house as good as new.

Then we all had pizza.

And we made a big mess!